# 50 THINGS YOU DIDN'T KNOW ABOUT AUSTRALIA

Written and Illustrated
by Sean O'Neill

Egremont, Massachusetts

**50 Things You Didn't Know About** is produced and published by Red Chair Press:
www.redchairpress.com

FREE lesson guide at www.redchairpress.com/free-activities

**Publisher's Cataloging-In-Publication Data**

*(Provided by Cassidy Cataloging Services, Inc)*

Names: O'Neill, Sean, 1968- author, illustrator. | O'Neill, Sean, 1968
50 things you didn't know about (Series)

Title: 50 things you didn't know about Australia / written and illustrated by Sean O'Neill.

Other Titles: Australia

Description: Egremont, Massachusetts : Red Chair Press, [2024] | Interest age level: 006-009. | Includes bibliographical references and index. | Summary: With 50 Things You Didn't Know About Australia, young readers will discover the highlights of Australia's ancient culture, modern cities, and discover unique aspects of food and daily life in this modern Continental nation.--Publisher.

Identifiers: ISBN: 978-1-64371-348-9 (library hardcover) | 978-1-64371-349-6 (softcover) | 978-1-64371-350-2 (ebook) | LCCN: 2023937072

Subjects: LCSH: Australia--History--Juvenile literature. | Australia--Description and travel--Juvenile literature. | Australia--Social life and customs--Juvenile literature. | CYAC: Australia--History. | Australia--Description and travel. | Australia--Social life and customs. | BISAC: JUVENILE NONFICTION / Travel. | JUVENILE NONFICTION / People & Places / Australia & Oceania.

Classification:LCC: DU96 .O54 2024 | DDC: 994--dc23



Printed in the United States of America

0524 1P F24CG

# TABLE of CONTENTS

CHAPTER 1

# AN ISLAND CONTINENT

An island unto itself, Australia is the only country on Earth that covers an entire continent (Oceania is a grouping but not itself a continent). Although it is the second-least populated continent (after Antarctica), the rich biodiversity and variety of ecosystems makes Australia one of the most unique natural environments on the planet. From arid deserts to sandy beaches, snow-capped mountains to bustling cities, Australia really is a place like no other.

**1** Australia isn't just a country. It's also a continent *and* an island. In fact, it's the world's smallest continent–and the world's largest island.

**2** The country's name comes from the Latin term *Terra Australis Incognita*, which means "unknown land in the south." European explorers used this term to identify any lands unknown to Europeans in the southern oceans, so when they landed on Australia, the name stuck.

3 Eastern Australia is separated from the rest of the continent by a large mountain range called the Great Dividing Range. It wasn't until 1813 that any settlers successfully crossed these mountains.

4 Much of central Australia, called the outback, is mostly desert. An area of southwestern Australia is called *Nullarbor* Plain for good reason. Nullarbor means "no trees" in Latin.

**5** The Australian outback is rich in minerals. The Argyle diamond mine in Kimberly produces more diamonds than any other mine in the world.

**6** Australia may be the world's smallest continent, but can claim to have the world's biggest rock. At 1,142 feet (348 meters) tall and 5.8 miles (9.3 km) around, Uluru is the world's biggest single rock.

**7** A very unusual rock formation with an even more unusual name is the Bungle Bungles in Western Australia. These beehive-shaped rocks are covered with orange and black stripes.

**8** The island state of Tasmania lies off the southern coast of Australia. It is the only place in the world where you find the fierce little mammal called the Tasmanian Devil.

**9** Another big difference from North America and Europe or much of Asia, is that because Australia is in the southern hemisphere, they experience summer when most of the world has winter, which can make for a very hot Christmas, Hanukkah, or New Year.

**10** Because it's an island, Australia is home to much wildlife that doesn't exist anywhere else in the world, including **marsupials** like kangaroos, wallabies, and koalas.

**11** Australians are definitely outnumbered by animals. There's a population of about 20 million people there, but close to 25 million kangaroos, and 120 million sheep!

**12** Kangaroos in the wild are known for boxing—for real! Male kangaroos, in order to establish dominance, will fight each other balancing on their large tails while kicking and punching an opponent.

**13** One of the most unusual animals found in Australia is the duck-billed platypus. It lives in the water, has the body of an otter, a tail like a beaver, and a bill like a duck. And, although it's a **mammal**, the platypus lays eggs like a bird!

**14** The platypus is so unusual that when the first example of the animal was sent from Australia to England, scientists at the British Museum thought it had been sewn together from different animal parts as a joke.

**15** The Australian outback is very dry. So dry, in fact, that Lake Eyre in South Australia is completely empty. It's a large basin that fills only every few decades when there's a flood.

**16** Because of the desert climate, English settlers brought camels to Australia to help explore the desert and build railroads. The camels made themselves at home, and now over a million camels roam wild in the Australian bush.

**17** Australia is known for its beaches. There are 10,685 of them! If you visited one each day, it would take 29 years to see them all.

**18** One of Australia's most amazing natural wonders is the Great Barrier Reef. Not only is it the largest coral reef in the world, but, because coral is made by tiny sea creatures, it is the largest **ecosystem** anywhere on Earth.

**19** The Great Barrier Reef is so big, it can be seen by astronauts from outer space.

**20** Australia's beaches may be beautiful, but be careful! Some of the deadliest poisonous and venomous animals on Earth live there. Contact with the box jellyfish or the blue-ringed octopus can be deadly!

**21** As if that weren't bad enough, Australians also have to contend with the funnel-web spider, one of the deadliest spiders on Earth.

**22** If all that sounds bad, be sure to stay away from the saltwater crocodile. The world's largest **reptile**, it can grow to 23 feet (7 m) long and over 2,000 pounds (907 kg), and has a nasty bite with its 64 teeth.

CHAPTER 2

# EXPLORATION AND DISCOVERY

When European explorers began to arrive in Australia in the 17th Century, they found a land that appeared untouched by civilization. In reality, Australia had been inhabited by rich and complex native societies that had been living on the island for more than 40,000 years. These two cultures have learned to live together as one nation, but it hasn't always been a smooth transition.

**23** When European explorers arrived, there were already many people living in Australia. There were about 300,000 **indigenous** Australian people, called *Aborigines*, living on the continent at the time. The word *aboriginal* means "being the first of a kind in a region."

**24** Ancient aboriginal artists made some of the oldest art on Earth. Cave paintings of kangaroos and crocodiles have been found that are over 20,000 years old.

**25** Aborigine hunters became famous for their use of the *boomerang.* This ingenious weapon is curved so that, if it misses its prey, it will fly in a large arc and return to the hunter.

**26** The person most remembered for establishing Australia as a British colony is explorer Captain James Cook, who arrived in 1700, mapped the entire east coast, and claimed the continent for King George III of England.

**27** In the early days, Australia had very few English residents. England had another problem: too many English criminals and convicts. The British government solved both problems by shipping convicted criminals off to Australia!

**28** Many Australian farmers began raising sheep for wool, but the sheep were often hunted by *dingoes*–Australian wild dogs. In the 1800s, ranchers built the world‘s largest fence–3,307 miles (5,300 km) long!—to keep the dingoes out.

**29** You may have heard of the California Gold Rush, but did you know about the *Australian* Gold Rush? In 1851, Englishman Edward Hargraves discovered gold in Bathurst in southern Australia. Within weeks the gold rush was on!

**30** So many people came to Australia looking for gold, the population doubled in just ten years. In fact, in England some people would deliberately get arrested and convicted of crimes so they would be sent to Australia to try to strike it rich.

**31** Not only did Australia have its own gold rush, but, like the American West, it also had famous outlaws. Ned Kelly is considered a folk hero by Australians, but, much like Jesse James and Butch Cassidy, he was a bank robber who was eventually caught by police and hanged.

**32** The Trans-Australian Railway was built in 1917 to connect western and southern Australia. It was called "the Tea and Sugar" because so many people relied on its weekly visits for necessities like food and drinks.

**33** It wasn't until 1860 that the first European Australians attempted to cross the entire continent. Robert O'Hara Burke and William John Wills made it across, but didn't plan well and ran out of food on the way back. They died of starvation.

CHAPTER 3

# A NEW NATION

The earliest European settlers in Australia were mostly from England, and for the first 100 years or so, Australia was a colony of the British Empire. But as the country grew, a strong national character emerged, the people of Australia began to form their own unique identity, and the desire to form an independent nation slowly took hold.

**34** By 1860, more than a million Europeans lived in Australia, but it was still a British colony. This ended in 1901, when the nation of Australia was officially formed at a celebration in Sydney.

**35** Although Australia is an independent nation, it remains a British commonwealth, which means it has a special relationship with Great Britain, and the people of Australia are still considered British subjects.

**36** Because it is a British commonwealth, the King of England is officially also the King of Australia. But, in reality, the government is led by a Prime Minister.

**37** Australia's connection to Britain can be seen in its flag, which contains the British Union Jack as part of its design. The large, seven-pointed star represents the seven states and territories of Australia, and the smaller stars form the shape of the Southern Cross constellation.

**38** The Aboriginal people of Australia, who have often been made to feel like outsiders in their own land, have created their own flag. In the Aboriginal flag the black band represents the Aboriginal people, the red band is the land, and the yellow circle is the sun.

**39** Australia's capital city Canberra was built as a compromise. Residents of Sydney and Melbourne, Australia's two largest cities, both wanted to be the capital. Instead, a new city was built halfway between both cities.

**40** Many people around the world were introduced to the new nation of Australia during the 1956 Olympic Games, which were held in Melbourne. This was the first Olympics to be widely seen on television.

**41** The city of Melbourne was almost named Batmania. It was founded by a settler named John Batman, and he originally wanted to name it after himself.

**42** In 1902, Australia became the second country in the world to give women the right to vote, and in 2010, Australia elected its first female prime minister, Julia Eileen Gillard.

**43** Australia is such a large, spread-out country that it can be hard for people in remote areas to get basic needs like medical care. To solve this problem, the Royal Flying Doctor Service was formed in 1928 to fly doctors to treat patients throughout the country.

CHAPTER

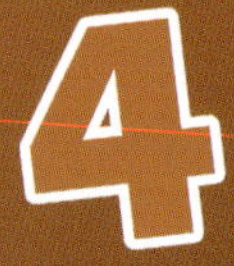

# DAILY LIFE

Although much of the Australian continent is covered in desert, about 90% of all Australians live in urban areas just a short distance from the ocean. Australia's large cosmopolitan cities are bustling and diverse, much like those in the United States or Europe. But Australians have a distinct style and character that is all their own.

**44** Australians refer to their country with the nickname "Oz," which means the people that live there are actually *Ozzies*, not *Aussies* as many people think.

**45** The official language of Australia is English, but Ozzies have their own unique way of speaking. Slang terms like "billabong," "jumbuck," "fair dinkum," and "strewth," can make it difficult for outsiders to understand.

**46** The large grazing plains of Australia are perfect for raising cattle, so, of course, there are plenty of cowboys, called *jackaroos*. As women began working with cattle they became known as–what else?—*jillaroos*!

**47** A national symbol of Australia is the famous Sydney Opera House. This architectural wonder is called the "coat hanger" by locals because of the sharp angles of its famous roof, which weighs in at 161,000 tons!

**48** A popular sport in Australia is Australian Rules Football. Similar in some ways to rugby or soccer, it's different from American football in one important way–no padding or helmets.

**49** A hero for many indigenous Australians was the Aboriginal tennis star Evonne Goolagong Cawley. She won the Australian Open Tennis competition four times, as well as Wimbledon and the French Open.

**50** Many American children enjoy a peanut-butter sandwich for lunch, but in Australia, lunch is a little different. A favorite sandwich down under is Vegemite, a salty paste made from brewer's yeast. Yum!

# Glossary

**ecosystem:** the interaction of all living things (animals, plants, insects) in an area with the non-living (water, dirt, stone, sun).

**indigenous:** people whose ancestors lived in a place from the earliest times.

**mammal:** a human or warm-blooded animal with a backbone.

**marsupials:** a group or type of mammal who carry their young in a pouch.

**reptiles:** cold-blooded animals with backbones and bodies covered in scales; mostly egg-laying.

# Explore More

**Mattern, Joanne.** *Animal Top 10: Most Dangerous (Earth's Amazing Animals)* Red Chair Press, 2020.

**Owings, Lisa.** *Learning About Australia.* Lerner Publications, 2016.

**Perkins, Chloe.** *Living in Australia (Ready-to-Read).* Simon Spotlight, 2017.

**Reynolds, A.M.** *Your Passport to Australia.* Capstone Press, 2022.

**Vallepur, Shalini.** *Australia (Where on Earth?).* Enslow, 2022.

# Index



## About the Author/Illustrator

**Sean O'Neill** is an illustrator and writer living in Chicago. He is the creator of *50 Things You Didn't Know* and the *Rocket Robinson* series of graphic novels. Sean loves history, trivia, and drawing cartoons, so this project is pretty much a dream assignment. And it comes with a fair dinkum of vegemite.